Ten Things About

Unanswered Prayer
&
How to Live with It

# Ten Things About

# Unanswered Prayer
# &
# How to Live with It

Reggie Weems

*Unless otherwise noted, Scripture quotations are taken from The Holy Bible, English Standard Version® (ESV®) Copyright © 2001 by Crossway, a publishing ministry of Good News Publishers. All rights reserved. ESV Text Edition: 2016*

Copyright © 2018, Reggie Weems
www.10thingsabout.org

All rights reserved. No part of this book may be reproduced, scanned, or distributed in any printed or electronic form without permission.

First Edition: 2018

ISBN 978-0-9996559-4-8

To buy quantities of this book at a special rate for bulk use, email
info@greatwriting.org

Great Writing Publications
www.greatwriting.org
Taylors, SC

# Table of Contents

About the Series and this Book ............... 9

Introduction ............................................. 11

1 The Importance of Prayer ..................... 17

2 Examples of Unanswered Prayer .......... 25

3 Let's Define Prayer ................................ 31

4 Ten Reasons for Unanswered Prayer ... 35

5 Ten Things about Living
  with Unanswered Prayer ..................... 49

6 Praying the ACTS Way .......................... 67

7 One More Thought ................................ 75

8 Conclusion ............................................. 79

About the Author ..................................... 85

In memory of Theodore Gschwind

and

in honor of the God who is still
answering his prayers

# About the Series and this Book

**TEN THINGS** is a series of books offering biblical encouragement and practical direction on matters of concern to modern Christians who are seeking Bible-saturated, Christ-centered, Spirit-empowered, practical guidance. The series is published in an electronic and print format for quick, private, and easy access.

The books are brief and to the point, enabling readers to access immediate help and genuine hope for real-life situations. They are also written in a pastoral tone intended to shepherd hearts and minds toward Christ-centered, whole-life transformation.

This encouragement is not intended to and cannot replace personal pastoral counsel or the accountability of living transparently in Christian fellowship with other believers. Both are invaluable to you. A particular book may inspire a reader, but lifelong change only occurs in the context of living in biblical community.

Because of its biblical and simple approach, pastors may also employ the series to disciple church leaders who minister to God's flock.

# Introduction

Theodore Gschwind became a Christian at the age of twenty-eight while working for the Los Angeles Times in California. His conversion is recounted simply in that single sentence. But there was nothing simple or conventional about Ted—the life he lived before his conversion or the manner in which he became a Christian and his life thereafter. He was an extraordinary man, disguised as an ordinary person who dressed each day in a dark blue suit and tie, regardless of the day's activities. I know he changed his own car oil in that suit and tie. I think he may even have swum in them! After his conversion, Ted began ministering in jails, a ministry he continued into his eighties. He once evangelized a death row convict who was later miraculously paroled and became a well-known pastor in El Paso, Texas. He also claimed that, in a twist on Hebrews 13:2, an angel repeatedly met him on the streets of Los Angeles and took him to a restaurant to feed him during the Great Depression.

I met Ted in my first pastorate, then a seventy-six-year-old, widowed deacon. Each week for the ten years of that freshman ministry, Ted and I met weekly for lunch as he poured himself into my life. Long before I met Ted, he was already praying for family members whom he longed to see come to faith in Christ. Throughout that decade, he and I repeatedly prayed together weekly for his same personal, heart-wrenching requests. Ted recognized that he was an older man and wondered if God would answer his prayers before he died. But amazingly, he was never discouraged by unanswered prayer. He had a good precedent for faithfully interceding, even if he didn't see the results of his prayers before he met Jesus face to face.

Ted considered himself a miracle at birth and rebirth. Before his conversion, a woman whom he affectionately referred to simply as sister Swihart not only prayed for him but let him know that she was praying for his salvation. Seemingly unaffected, Ted continued living his brashly public, ungodly life. His wife, Edna, repeatedly locked him out of the house after drunken brawls. His son, David, recounts the day his unemployed, unconverted, "baby-sitting" father sat him on the bar of the local beer joint and ordered his four-year-old son a root beer. And then sister Swihart died… and Ted was not a Christian. But several years after her death, God wonderfully saved Ted and he spent the rest of his life passionately exacting revenge on his unconverted years. When I met him, he showed no signs of slowing down.

Of the many stories Ted shared in that decade of mentoring a young pastor, the story about God's unanswered prayer has remained with me the most. Ted told everyone, literally everyone, about his miraculous conversion, and he never told the story without saying that he was "the product of sister Swihart's unanswered prayer." It was the paradoxical catch phrase he used to get people's attention so he could tell the whole tale and share Jesus with his intrigued audience. That story still inspires me as I struggle with unanswered prayers. I hope it will encourage you, as you pray in "the assurance of things hoped for, the conviction of things not seen" (Hebrews 11:1).

# Action Points

1. Even before you begin the book, you may want to make a list of those heart-wrenching petitions you regularly bring before God. If you don't have a prayer journal, you could write them here.

_____

_____

2. Read Jeremiah 32:17 in which Jeremiah confesses, "Nothing is too hard for you." What did Jeremiah confess about God in the first portion of that verse that brought him to that conclusion?

_____

_____

3. Now read verses 18-22. God's past faithfulness to Israel encouraged Jeremiah's prayers. Take a few moments to review God's faithful-

ness to you. Write those experiences in the space following or in your journal.

_____

_____

4 Write down some examples of God's greatness revealed in Israel's history and your personal life. The biblical model is to think about God before we petition him. This keeps your prayer life from becoming a review of problems, and highlights God's ability to accomplish what you might otherwise consider impossible.

_____

_____

5. Think about the stories you personally know of unanswered prayer being answered. Write one or two of them here.

_____

_____

_____

# 1

The Importance of Prayer

Prayer is a unique privilege. By it, you have access to the one, true, living God. He has invited you into his throne room "that we may receive mercy and find grace to help in time of need" (Hebrews 4:16). No honor in life compares to prayer and there are many reasons it is so important.

Prayer is important because in prayer you acknowledge your sin, repent of it, and trust in Jesus as your Savior. This is true of all people everywhere and it is the only way to be saved. (Romans 10:12; Ephesians 2:18).

Prayer is also one of the greatest evidences you are a Christian. Every child naturally loves his or her parent. Romans 8:15 states that God has given you "the Spirit of adoption as sons, by whom we cry, 'Abba! Father!'" You were created for fellowship with God and he intends you to live in community with him. Prayer is the desire and delight of every true believer. If you really are, whatever you are in private, prayer gives you the assurance you are genuinely born again.

Prayer is so important to the vitality of your Christian life that Paul commands you to "pray without ceasing" (1 Thessalonians 5:17). This is because prayer is to a Christian what breath is to a human. Prayer is the oxygen of your spiritual life. If you neglect prayer, you impoverish your own soul. As a Christian, prayer should be your first priority and not a last resort. Prayer should be the undertone of your life—as you rise in the morning, go about your day, and as you go to sleep at night.

You can rest assured that that when you are unable to pray about something or are unclear about what to pray, the Holy Spirit is praying for you. Romans 8:26 teaches us that "the Spirit helps us in our weakness. For we do not know what to pray for as we ought, but the Spirit himself intercedes for us with groanings too deep for words." You have undoubtedly experienced those deep groanings of inexpressible words and emotions.

Incredibly, the next verse in that passage also indicates that if you are praying amiss, the Holy Spirit will even correct your inaccurate prayers. Paul wrote: "And he who searches hearts knows what is the mind of the Spirit because the Spirit intercedes for the saints according to the will of God" (Romans 8:27). As we intercede in prayer, the Holy Spirit will redirect our prayers to ensure we are praying "according to the will of God." That's an amazing promise when we apply it to how we pray today.

Years ago, a woman who had regularly prayed for me died. I lamented her loss to a friend who reminded me that you and I have an ever-living prayer partner in Jesus. Hebrews 7:25 tells you that "he [Jesus] is able to save to the uttermost those who draw near to God through him, since he always lives to make intercession for them." Did you get that? Jesus lives to pray for you. He is your most intimate, faithful, and powerful prayer partner.

Prayer is so important to your Christian life that you must also be careful about prayerlessness, which is a source of ungodliness. In the Garden of Gethsemane, Jesus warned the disciples that prayer was the antidote to temptation (Luke 22:40). But the disciples failed to "watch and pray" (Mathew 26:41) with Jesus. Immediately afterward, Peter erroneously attempted to bring God's kingdom to earth by the sword and was severely rebuked by Jesus who also reversed Peter's actions (Luke 22:47-51).

Prayer is also an extremely important discipline for the local church. In Isaiah 56:6-8, God called his "holy Mountain" a place of prayer for all nations. In the New Testament, Jesus claimed the gathering place of Christians as a "house of prayer" (Matthew 21:3). In response, the newly founded church exercised prayer as one of four disciplines (Acts 2:24) and the early church made prayer a priority (Acts 1:13-14, 4:23-31, 12:12). Prayer was so important to the elders of the church in Jerusalem that they went to great lengths to ensure they could devote themselves "to prayer and to the ministry of the word" (Acts 6:4).

# Action Points

1. Write the references for those Scriptures that most encourage you to pray.

_____

_____

2. Write down several of these so that God can encourage you when you pray. You can also meditate on these verses when Satan discourages you about God's faithfulness.

_____

_____

3. Reflect on Hebrews 7:25. In what ways does the idea of Jesus as your prayer partner encourage your prayer life?

_____

_____

4. What did you learn in this chapter about the danger of prayerlessness? How does it encourage you to pray?

_____

_____

5. What can you do to encourage intercessory prayer in your church body? Could God use you to emphasize corporate prayer, to revitalize prayer in small groups or to encourage people with unanswered prayer requests to gather regularly for prayer?

_____

_____

_____

_____

THINK ABOUT IT

Prayer is to your spiritual life what
breath is to your natural life.

# 2

## Examples of Unanswered Prayer

Of course, one of your great encouragements to pray is that Jesus repeatedly promised to answer your prayers (Matthew 7:7; 21:22; Mark 11:24; John 14:13-14; John 16:23; 1 John 5:14-15). It is because of the high expectations you have about prayer that unanswered prayer is so painful. With so many promises of prayer being answered, you naturally expect the door to be open and for God to hear and answer your prayers. The last thing you expect is for the heavens to be brass (Deuteronomy 28:23), reflecting only the sound of your voice. But there are reasons for unanswered prayer. Once you remind yourself about who God is and what he is doing in your world, you can learn to live contentedly with unanswered prayer.

When I think of unanswered prayer, my mind races to Hannah who "year by year" went to the Temple to pray for a child (1 Samuel 1:7-8). I think about Habakkuk who cried "O LORD, how long shall I cry for help, and you will not hear? Or cry to you 'Violence!' and you will not save?" (Habakkuk 1:2). The example I will use in this book is the prayer of Mary and Martha on behalf of their brother Lazarus (John 11:3). The reason I have chosen to do so is because the death of a loved one is often most grievous unanswered prayer.

But, of course, the most important and mind-boggling unanswered prayer in the Bible is that of Jesus, when on the cross, he cried, "My God, my God, why have you forsaken me?" (Matthew 27:46). Although it's not part of our discussion, the example of Jesus provides many answers to the question of unanswered prayer. In that particular case, the Father did not answer his son so that he could answer you. He did not save his son so that he could save you. This reality certainly makes us think harder and longer about unanswered prayer. We'll talk more about that later.

For now, please remember that if you are enduring unanswered prayer, Jesus has endured that experience and is not oblivious to your sorrow (Hebrews 4:14-16). The writer of Hebrews offers Jesus' intercessory ministry as one reason we should not lose hope or faith as we pray. He writes, "Since then we have a great high priest who has passed through the heavens, Jesus, the Son of God, let us hold fast our confession" (Hebrews 4:14). May Christ's example and words encourage you.

One last thing: in reality, God answers all prayer. His answers can be qualified as "yes," "no," and "wait." If your prayers are not answered with a "yes," the (un)answer is either "no" or "wait." And you often can't tell the difference between "wait" and "no." But as you will soon see from the pages of Scripture, unanswered prayer, be it "wait" or "no," is often God's better answer.

# Action Points

1. Make a list of Jesus' prayer promises.

_____

_____

2. Read the accounts of Hannah and Habakkuk and see how you may find hope in how they lived with unanswered prayer.

_____

3. Read Hebrews 4:14-16 and then think about Jesus' prayer on the cross. God did not answer his dying prayer but, of course, that was not the end of the story! How does that unanswered prayer make Jesus a wonderful counselor and intercessor?

_____

_____

## THINK ABOUT IT

God answers every prayer. Even though it may be more difficult to accept, sometimes "wait" or "no" is the best answer.

# 3

Let's Define Prayer

To better understand unanswered prayer, let's first define the term prayer. The single English word for "prayer" is translated from various different Greek words. For instance,

- *Aiteo* means to ask with urgency (John 16:26; James 1:5-6).
- *Deomai* means to beg (Matthew 1:34; Galatians 4:12).
- *Deeis* refers to request for a need (Luke 1:13; 2 Timothy 1:3).
- *Epikaleo* means to call and express confession (Acts 9:13-14; Philippians 4:6).
- *Erotao* means to beg (John 12:21; 2 Corinthians 12:8).
- *Krazo* is a cry for help (Romans 8:15-16; Galatians 4:6).
- *Euchomai* means to vow (Romans 9:3; 2 Corinthians 13:7).
- *Proseuche* is a more general word for prayer and is used only of prayer to God (Matthew 17:21; Revelation 5:8).

*Proseuche* is the word most commonly translated "prayer" in the New Testament and, as that specific word, it occurs 37 times in the New Testament. However, it appears about 127 times in its various derivatives. *Proseuche* is a compound word taken from the preposition *pros*, meaning *with* or *toward* and the noun *euche*, meaning *wish, desire* or *vow*. As such, prayer accomplishes at least two things: it moves you *toward* God, bringing you closer *with* him, and it causes you to *vow* love, obedience and surrender to God. In other words, prayer changes you as much as it changes anything you request. And, in effect, unanswered prayer does those things as well. But unanswered prayer is a unique pain. After all, if God is great and God is good (and he is both simultaneously), why do your prayers go unanswered?

Before we talk about how to live with unanswered prayer, here are ten reasons why you may be enduring unanswered prayer. I hope each of them will provide you with an opportunity for reflection about God, yourself, and your relationship to him.

# 4

Ten Reasons for
Unanswered Prayer

# ONE

God may not answer your prayer because you prefer sin to God. The writer of Psalm 66 understood "If I had cherished iniquity in my heart, the Lord would not have listened" (v. 18). Your relationship with God forms the basis for prayer. A broken relationship impedes answered prayer. If you prefer sin to God, he will not answer your prayer, in part to teach you that he is more important than anything else in life. Indeed, the Blesser is the host of all blessings.

# TWO

God may not answer your prayer because your requests are inconsistent with his character. Jesus told the disciples, "Whatever you ask in my name, this I will do, that the Father may be glorified in the Son" (John 14:13). The phrase, "God can do anything" is actually shorthand for the reality that God can and will do anything that is consistent with his nature. For instance, God cannot lie, etc. Answered prayer is a reflection of God. If you ask something that will discredit God's true nature, he will not answer it affirmatively.

# THREE

God may not answer your prayer because it is not in his will to do so. This is what it means to pray in Jesus' name. In John 14:14 Jesus promised, "If you ask me anything in my name, I will do it." Praying in Jesus name' means asking for things that are consistent with God's will. Someone said, "God's will is what we would choose every time if only we knew better." God is too good to give you anything less than his will.

# FOUR

God may not answer your prayer because we are praying selfishly. James warns, "You ask and do not receive, because you ask wrongly…" and in this case, the text interprets "wrongly" to mean "to spend it on your passions" (James 4:3). God is not Santa Claus. Nor is he a celestial bellhop. Omnipotence does not bend to your will or to your purposes. Prayer is a God-centered and God-glorifying exercise. Because God is good, all he intends is for your good. But God's glory is your greatest good and he will not let you waste the great privilege of prayer on selfish ends.

# FIVE

God may not answer your prayer because you have asked for something that will harm you. God knows what is best for you and his goodness may refuse your prayers. God always desired to have a special relationship with Israel in which he was the divine king of his chosen people. But Israel rejected the Lord's rule and asked for an earthly king (1 Samuel 8:7). After God detailed the selfishness a human king would exercise, he warned the nation, "And in that day you will cry out because of your king, whom you have chosen for yourselves, but the LORD will not answer you in that day" (1 Samuel 8:18). God loves you too much to satisfy a request that will hurt you.

# SIX

God may not answer your prayer because he is redirecting your life. In Acts 16, the apostle Paul wanted to take the gospel into Bithynia "but the Spirit of Jesus did not allow" him to do so (v. 7). Instead, Paul went to Troas. There, he received a vision of a man "urging him to 'Come over to Macedonia and help us'" (Acts 16:9). The "no" concerning Bithynia resulted in ministry in Macedonia: the conversion of Lydia, her house, the Philippian jailer, his house, and the establishment of the church in Philippi as a beachhead in modern-day Europe. There is a sense in which every Western Christian owes his or her salvation to God's "no" to Paul concerning Bithynia.

# SEVEN

God may not answer your prayer because he has the bigger picture in mind. You may want God to answer you on a micro level but God is working on a macro level. You naturally think about yourself when God is thinking on a larger scale. You want God to do one thing or affect one person when God intends to do many things and affect many people. Consider Jesus' cry from the cross, "My God, my God, why have you forsaken me?" (Matthew 27:46). Scripture does not record any answer to his prayer. But Jesus' rescue would have meant your damnation. God's "no" to Jesus' cry means "yes" when you ask God to save you. You may want an immediate, short-term answer when God is planning a more long-term, transforming response.

# EIGHT

God may not answer your prayer because he is concerned about your holiness more than your happiness. The apostle Paul learned this lesson. He writes, "Three times I pleaded with the Lord about this, that it should leave me. But he said to me, 'My grace is sufficient for you, for my power is made perfect in weakness'" (2 Corinthians 12:8-9a). In this context, God's "no" to Paul about physical healing led to a spiritual revelation. As a result, he experienced God's sufficient grace, perfecting power, supernatural contentment, and divine strength. He concluded: "Therefore I will boast all the more gladly of my weaknesses, so that the power of Christ may rest upon me. For the sake of Christ, then, I am content with weaknesses, insults, hardships, persecutions, and calamities. For when I am weak, then I am strong" (vs 9b-10). Paul's unanswered prayer led to a new level of holiness in his life and this, in turn, increased his joy.

# NINE

God may not answer your prayer because unanswered prayer leads to greater influence. After Elijah's exhausting encounter with Jezebel, he ran for his life and prayed, "'It is enough; now, O LORD, take away my life...'" (1 Kings 19:4). But God was not finished with Elijah. He didn't answer Elijah's prayer because he intended to multiply Elijah's sphere of influence. The prophet later anointed Jehu as king of Israel, he prophesied about the deaths of Ahab, Jezebel, and Ahaziah (Ahab's son), and was taken to heaven in a whirlwind. He also anointed his successor, Elisha, whose ministry was five years longer than his had been and who performed twice as many miracles as his mentor.

## TEN

God may not answer your prayer because he has something better for you. This brings us to Mary, Martha, and Lazarus, the women's unanswered prayer on behalf of their brother, and ten things about living with unanswered prayer. You need to know these ten things because, in spite of all God intends for you through unanswered prayer, it is still one of the most excruciating pains you will ever endure. Let me encourage you to open your Bible to John 11:1-44 and read along as we walk through this passage about unanswered prayer.

Understanding why God may not answer prayer doesn't necessarily remove the pain of unanswered prayer. Like Hannah, Habakkuk, Mary, Martha, and even the Lord Jesus, you still have to travel through that dark valley of sorrow. And that brings us to direction and encouragement about living with unanswered prayer.

## THINK ABOUT IT

There are many reasons God does not answer prayer with a "yes." Because God is good and great, unanswered prayer, although painful, is always in our best interest.

# Action Points

1. Think about these ten reasons. Is sin a barrier in your prayer life? If so, take time now to confess your sin, ask God for forgiveness, and revel in his mercy. Write your prayer here.

_____

_____

2. Think deeply about God's character and will for your life. Is your prayer consistent with who God is and what he is doing in the world? Are your prayers more about you and your personal happiness than God's glory? Take time to reflect on that issue and reorient your prayers accordingly. Write your prayer here.

_____

_____

3. Perhaps God is using unanswered prayer to point out idol worship in your life. Are you genuinely trusting God, and can you be satisfied with him more than the answers to prayer? It may take some time to reflect on this issue but it is well invested time. What might you be valuing more than God? Write that answer here.

_____

_____

4. Who is your God, i.e., what makes you happy and fulfilled: your answered prayers or God himself?

_____

_____

And now, here are ten things on which to meditate. As you do, I hope God will answer your prayer about unanswered prayer.

# 5

Ten Things about Living with
Unanswered Prayer

I know that you are anxious to talk about living with answered prayer. But defining prayer and reflecting on the possible reasons for unanswered prayer are essential stepping stones to that discussion. Hopefully God has used these previous pages to prepare your heart for what comes next. Here are ten pillars on which to build a foundation of hope and joy in the world of unanswered prayer.

# ONE

God knows your need before you ask. In John 11:3, Mary and Martha sent word to Jesus saying, "Lord, he whom you love is ill." This news was new to Jesus' disciples but not to Jesus. He knew Lazarus was ill before messengers from Bethany reached him at the Jordan river, east of Jericho, approximately fifteen miles northeast of Bethany. At that time, Jesus also prophesied the consequence of Lazarus' illness. If you look closely at the text, you will note that Lazarus' sisters really didn't ask Jesus to come to Bethany or heal Lazarus from a distance. They didn't request anything at all. They simply wanted Jesus to know that the friend whom he loved was dying (v. 3). They surmised that it would be enough for Jesus to know. And it is. To remember that God knows, gives you rest, peace, and hope, God knew of the reason for your prayers before the need existed. He also knows the outcome. Knowing that God knows will sustain you as wait for God to answer or wonder why he has said 'no.'

# TWO

Of course, just knowing that God knows your dilemma isn't the answer you seek. But look closely at the sisters' message to Jesus. It didn't simply contain information. They specifically said, "Lord, he whom you love is ill." The understanding that Jesus loved Lazarus changed everything about the sisters' request. Lazarus wasn't a stranger to Jesus. Nor was he a simple acquaintance. Jesus loved Lazarus, so much so that it was evident to Mary and Martha and to the disciples also. You know this because John, the narrator, confirms that "Jesus loved Martha and her sister and Lazarus" (v. 5). Knowing that God loves you doesn't answer your prayer but it does lift your downcast heart in the midst of unanswered prayer. It reminds you that God is working for you and for your good. His love for you does not entertain ill will. Whatever happens, God's love for you is the one, single, unchangeable reality that changes everything.

# THREE

Remember also that unanswered prayer doesn't mean to God what it means to us. Lazarus' sisters believed their brother would die if Jesus didn't arrive in time. A personal, immediate resurrection never occurred to them. But Jesus knew "this illness does not lead to death" (v. 4). He acknowledged a difference between what he called "sleeping" (v. 11) and death (v. 14). Yet we know that Lazarus died. This means Jesus interpreted the situation differently than Mary, Martha or the disciples. He did so because he is the resurrection (v. 25) and this gives death a different meaning to God. Jesus' resurrection also gives us a different perspective. Your tendency may be to misinterpret unanswered prayer. But don't let what you *don't* know take precedence over what you *do* know. You do know God. You do know God's intention in everything. Rest in what you do know while you wrestle with what you don't know.

# FOUR

The Bible frequently confirms that God's glory is our greatest good. When Jesus heard that Lazarus was sick, he informed the disciples that Lazarus' illness "is for the glory of God, that the Son of God may be glorified through it" (v. 4). God's glory and your good are not antonyms but synonyms. Loving, honoring, and obeying God maintained the Garden of Eden. Adam and Eve's disobedience turned he world into a wasteland. Glorifying God is our greatest good because our good is wrapped up in God's glory. Everything God does is for his own glory. And he is too glorious not to be glorified. In the end, he wins! We win with him because his glory secures our good. Do your best to keep this in mind as you struggle with unanswered prayer. Everything is intended to (and ultimately will) glorify God which, in turn, ensures that your greatest good is served.

# FIVE

Lazarus' death also reminds you that God's delays are not necessarily denials. When Jesus heard "that Lazarus was ill, he stayed two days longer in the place where he was" (v. 6). By doing so, Jesus is intentionally impressing the time delay on the sisters and the disciples. John records it to intentionally impress the time delay on you. But the wait doesn't mean that Jesus denied the sisters' implied request to help Lazarus. Instead, the resurrection of a person four-days-dead will generate faith for many people (v. 45).

Remember, when you are waiting, God is working. You may not see what he is doing but he is always working and his timing is always perfect. Even "no" will one day become "yes" because "all the promises of God find their Yes in him" (2 Corinthians 1:20). Like the day Lazarus was resurrected, a day is coming in which every one of your prayers will be answered "yes," beyond your wildest expectations.

# SIX

When Jesus did begin the journey to Judea where Bethany was located, the disciples were surprised. Jesus had only recently left that region and the disciples queried "Rabbi, the Jews were just now seeking to stone you, and are you going there again?" (v. 8). This is an amazing thought that you shouldn't miss. Bethany is only two miles from Jerusalem—the seat of animosity toward Jesus and the place he would eventually be crucified. His return to Bethany placed Jesus in danger. In fact, John records, "So from that day on they made plans to put him to death" (v. 53). Unanswered prayer may grieve you but Jesus' compassion on a family in Bethany led him to pray the only unanswered prayer he ever uttered. God knows. God understands. He is not indifferent. And Jesus sympathizes with your weakness because he has been likewise tempted (Hebrews 4:15).

# SEVEN

The reason Jesus gave the disciples for returning to Bethany was, "Our friend Lazarus has fallen asleep, but I go to awaken him" (v. 11). Jesus meant that Lazarus had died but the disciples "thought that he meant taking rest in sleep" (v. 13). At that point "Jesus told them plainly, 'Lazarus has died." (v. 14). During his earthly ministry, the disciples often misinterpreted Jesus' statements and actions. Crises often confuse our thinking. We think one thing; God intends another. This can be true of unanswered prayer, which we misinterpret as Jesus' lack of knowledge, care or ability. But God's thoughts and ways are "higher than your ways…and thoughts" (Isaiah 55:8-9). To endure unanswered prayer, you will have to trust the God you know as revealed in the Jesus who has saved you. You may not know many answers to many things. But you know God. And for people like Job, who endured his own unanswered prayers, God is answer enough (Job 42:1-6).

# EIGHT

Amazingly, Jesus said, "and for your sake I am glad that I was not there, so that you may believe" (v. 15). As such, unanswered prayer is meant to increase, not decrease, our faith. The disciples had already seen Jesus heal sick people, Peter's mother-in-law, included. But they had never seen him raise a man from the dead who had been dead for four days (v. 39). They knew Jesus as the one "who opened the eyes of the blind man" and it's true that he could "also have kept this man from dying" (v. 36). But that would not have accomplished what the disciples, Mary, and Martha needed most. What they needed most was to know that Jesus was the resurrection. This wasn't a future hope as Martha supposed it to be (v. 24). At Bethany, Jesus made it personal and immediate. The Jesus who stood before Martha was "the resurrection and the life" (v. 25). "Whoever believes in me," Jesus said, "though he die, yet shall he live and everyone who lives and believes in me shall never die"

(vv. 26-27). There are occasions when unanswered prayer enables us to experience more than answered prayer. To you, death is death. To Jesus, death is life—so much so, that God "is not the God of the dead, but of the living" (Mark 12:27). And this hope helps us live with unanswered prayer.

# NINE

In the end, Martha's unanswered prayer saved her. Prior to Lazarus' death, she had known and befriended Jesus. But until Lazarus' resurrection, she had never seen him as her Savior. When Jesus asked, "Do you believe this?" (v. 26) Martha responded, "Yes, Lord; I believe that you are the Christ, the Son of God…" (v. 27).

The Bible is replete with references to suffering people whose unanswered prayers lead them to the saving sufficiency of Jesus. Think about Jonah who cried from the belly of a great fish that Jesus said foreshadowed his own death: "'Salvation belongs to the LORD!'" (Jonah 2:9). God's great end is not this life. Nor is it everything this life can afford. This life is such a vapor that when God creates a "new heavens and new earth…the former things shall not be remembered or come into mind" (Isaiah 65:17). It is no wonder that "What no eye has seen, what no hear has heard, and what no human mind has conceived—the things

God has prepared for those who love him" (1 Corinthians 2:9).

Until then, your good God is using everything that occurs in your life to work toward that ultimate end. God is preparing a new people to live in that new creation and you are one of those people. In the interim, everything works together for your eternal good (Romans 8:28, 30). Until then, nothing can separate you from his love (Romans 8:31-38). God has saved you from his wrath. He is saving you from the flesh, the world, and the devil. Just as in Martha's life, even unanswered prayer, is saving you

# TEN

Interestingly, the Bible never records a single word that Lazarus spoke. But his voice is not silent. In its place, Jesus "cried with a loud voice, 'Lazarus, come out'" (v. 43). Lazarus' death and resurrection speaks more than his life ever did. The same can be true of unanswered prayer. In Jesus' resurrection, God still speaks powerfully today. He speaks to our suffering and sorrow in his cross. He answers our questions in his death and resurrection. All we really need to know is found in the words "It is finished" (John 19:30) and "He is not here; he has risen, just as he said" (Matthew 28:6).

In creation, God is the first word. At the empty tomb, He is the last word. And "not the smallest letter, not the least stroke of a pen, will by any means disappear…until everything is accomplished" (Matthew 5:18). He is not simply the great Author but the great Finisher as well (Hebrews 12:2). What he has begun in you and in this world, he will complete (Philippians 1:6). Not even death can keep him from keeping his promise or keep you from his promise.

This brings us full circle. Earlier I mentioned the reason for choosing the story of Lazarus is because the death of a loved one is commonly the most sorrowful of unanswered prayers. But John 11 demonstrates that Jesus' resurrection is our resurrection. In that scenario, what appears to be an unanswered prayer is God's greatest answer to prayer.

# Action Points

1. What great truths struck your heart as you read this list of ten things about unanswered prayer? Write those thoughts here.

_____

_____

_____

2. Is there a particular number in the list that is personal to you? Let me encourage you to rewrite it here as an expression of your understanding of what God is doing through unanswered prayer.

_____

_____

_____

_____

## THINK ABOUT IT

Mary and Martha's unanswered prayer preceded the resurrection of Lazarus. God's "no" was the most life-transforming answer for all three of them.

# 6

Praying the ACTS Way

Just before we finish, it might be helpful to think about the structure of your prayer life. There are innumerable models for constructing your prayer life. Several years ago, I was privileged to write a book titled, *On Wings of Prayer: Praying the ACTS Way*[1]. ACTS is a simple acrostic for Adoration, Confession, Thanksgiving, and Supplication. But if you'll look at it closely, ACTS can prioritize your prayer life in a way that is beneficial to your struggle with unanswered prayer.

Think about it. The greater part of our prayer lives is consumed with petition. But if your prayer life is nothing but requests, it really amounts to a constant review of your problems. That alone is discouraging. Praying the *ACTS* way not only shapes your prayers but directs your prayer life. I want to encourage you to consider deploying this prayer model in your own life. It will take more time than just petitioning God in a moment of cri-

---

[1] Day One Publications, Leominster, England, 2009

sis but the time to create a biblical prayer life will be a reward in itself. It will also help you maintain a prayer life for a lifetime and especially as you live with unanswered prayer.

The pattern for ACTS is found in several passages of Scripture but let's use Daniel 9 for an example. Turn there in your Bible and be a Berean to "see if these things" are so (Acts 17:11).

You know the story behind Daniel's life. He was kidnapped as a teenager by Nebuchadnezzar and transported from Judah to Babylon where he successfully lived through the monarchies of several kings, endured many trials, was given a series of prophetic visions, and eventually became a high-ranking official in several empires. But throughout it all, Daniel's heart remained committed to God, Israel, and the restoration of God's people to the Promised Land. The last mention of Daniel in the book that bears his name is during the third year of King Cyrus. This means Daniel went into captivity between the ages of 14 and 20 and died between 85 and 90.

Scripture teaches that Daniel had a regular prayer life, apparently praying three times each day (Daniel 6:10) and chapter 9 presents a pattern he may have regularly employed. This is what it looks like:

- Verses 3-4 — **A**doration — This is who God is
- Verses 5-11 — **C**onfession — This is the sin you have committed
- Verses 12-15 — **T**hanksgiving — This is a record of God's work in the past
- Verses 16-19 — **S**upplication — This is what you are asking God to do

Now, think about your prayer life in its real context. If you are like many Christians, the majority of your prayer time is consumed by the recitation of your problems. That can be very discouraging. Notice that Daniel prefaces his petition with at least three other priorities. His petitions comprise only four of seventeen verses.

Before Daniel ever asked God for anything, he reminded himself of who God is, how great he is (vv. 3–4), and remembered how God had previously kept his word (vv. 12–15). In this case, sadly, Daniel recounted God's faithfulness to judge Israel and Judah because of their sin. His point, nonetheless, was to remember God's faithfulness to his word and Israel.

This model encourages your prayer life and keeps you from discouragement by placing God's greatness and faithfulness alongside your petitions. Making God great in prayer reminds you how big God is compared to the problems and sorrows of your life. Confessing our sin and acknowledging God's forgiveness also encourages you to remember the power of the cross and God's faithfulness to his word (1 John 1:9). Thanksgiving parades God's former goodness. If you use this model, by the time you get to your supplications, you will bring a good and great God to the table of that discussion. This alone can encourage you in innumerable ways as you live with unanswered prayer. Let me encourage you to try it right now.

# Action Points

1. Make a list of words that describe God. Consider using Bible terms for God. Ensure the list contains personal examples of God's goodness and greatness to you. Use this space but in the future, consider a prayer journal for using *ACTS*.

_____

_____

2. Confess your sin to God and thank him for his forgiveness. What Scriptures might you use to acknowledge your sin and remember God's salvation? Consider reading Psalms 32 and 51 and memorizing Psalm 32:1, 5 and Psalm 51:1–2.

_____

_____

_____

3. Review God's faithfulness to you in the past. Make a list of the times and things God has done and for which you are thankful. Here's room to do so but, again, consider a prayer journal.

_____

_____

4. Write your petitions in the space provided. For the purposes of this exercise, look closely at your lists of God's goodness, forgiveness, and thankfulness when compared to your list of petitions.

_____

_____

_____

Employing ACTS will encourage you as you live with unanswered prayer. Again, it's only one model and you may already be using a template that works for you. But if not, consider ACTS. Whatever you do, don't let supplication be the only or largest part of your prayer life.

## THINK ABOUT IT

Adoration, confession, thanksgiving, and petition are all equally important aspects of prayer. A balanced prayer life creates a healthy life.

# 7

One More Thought

At his most desperate hour Jesus surrounded himself with people whom he called to pray with him (Matthew 26:36-46). The book of Daniel reminds us that he, Daniel, was not exiled alone (Daniel 1:6). I want to encourage you to enlist others to pray with you and for you about your unanswered prayers. Don't take that counsel lightly.

God lives in the eternal community of the Trinity and is creating a family to live with him forever. Isolation and Christianity are oxymoronic, as is anonymous Christianity. Except in the most extreme cases, there is no such thing as a lone Christian. And even in prison, Paul surrounded himself with friends and asked others to join him (2 Timothy 4:9-13).

Think about people who could support you. Pray and ask God to open your heart and their hearts to the possibility. Write their names in the space at the end of this chapter or in your journal:

Make the time to reach out to this person or these people. Set an appointment to ask about partnering with you in prayer. You may be shy about praying aloud in front of other people but, I guarantee you, everyone initially feels the same way. I learned to pray, in part, by listening to Ted Gschwind pray. You will also learn to pray and teach others to pray by praying with people. You will find praying together is a vital part of joyful and hopeful life.

_____

_____

_____

_____

_____

THINK ABOUT IT

Praying with others can teach you to
pray, give strength to your prayer life,
and keep you from despair. Take
advantage of the family God
has given you.

# 8

Conclusion

Before Ted died, God answered several his most passionate prayers about loved ones; but not all of them. I am happy to tell you that, since Ted's death, God continues to answer his prayers; but not all of them…yet. But I am not discouraged for him. Ted is the perfect example of unanswered, answered prayer.

This little book is intended only as a primer on the subject of unanswered prayer. No one but the person whose prayers are unanswered understands the agony of that experience. For many people, perhaps for you, it is an enduring pain. Though I have been concise, I have not intended to take lightly whatever sorrow you are enduring because of unanswered prayer. You may rest assured that I, and people whom I love, also suffer with you on this matter.

Our first encounter with God in the Old Testament reveals him as great—he created everything—and good—creation was "very good" when he finished (Genesis 1:31). Sin caused the human race to fall and that brokenness tempts us to question God's greatness and goodness. We ask, "Is God not great or good enough to answer my prayer?" Let me assure you, he is both. He is too great to be unable, and too good to do wrong by you.

The reason God does not answer prayer is because it is the best answer. God is synonymous with best; not good, not great, but best. He is the best God and he only does what is best. He also does not want you to settle for anything less than best. Everything that is and everything that happens is God's means to best. Stop and take the time to seriously think about it. Review the Bible and your own life. You know God is great. You know God is good. You know that unanswered prayer is in your best interest and in the best interests of those you love.

William Cowper (1731-1800) is one of my heroes. He qualifies as a hero because of his transparency about the pain he endured and the hope he found in the midst of unending sorrow. From the age of twenty-one, he suffered a lifelong struggle with depression—particularly four episodes, each more painful than the previous. His accumulating agony became so great that he attempted suicide on three occasions. In an effort to salvage his tormented life, Cowper's brother placed him in an asylum for the insane. There, Christ miraculously saved William Cowper. But eternal salvation did not rescue him from temporal torments. Yet years later, he endured what he called "the fatal dream," and was haunted by recurring doubts concerning his salvation.

Yet in the midst of Cowper's pain, God's grace enabled him to pen many well-known Christian hymns—*There is a Fountain Filled with Blood*, perhaps the most famous among them. He also wrote one of Christianity's most glorious poems—one that I hope will encourage your heart in the midst of your unanswered prayer. The poem, *God Moves in a Mysterious Way* reads:

> *God moves in a mysterious way*
> *His wonders to perform;*
> *He plants his footsteps in the sea,*
> *And rides upon the storm.*
>
> *Deep in unfathomable mines*
> *Of never failing skill,*
> *He treasures up his bright designs*
> *And works his sovereign will.*
>
> *Ye fearful saints, fresh courage take,*
> *The clouds ye so much dread*
> *Are big with mercy, and shall break*
> *In blessings on your head.*

*Judge not the Lord by feeble sense,*
*But trust him for his grace;*
*behind a frowning providence*
*He hides a smiling face.*

*His purposes will ripen fast,*
*Unfolding every hour;*
*The bud may have a bitter taste,*
*But sweet will be the flower.*

*Blind unbelief is sure to err,*
*And scan his work in vain:*
*God is his own interpreter,*
*And he will make it plain.*

# About the Author

**REGGIE WEEMS** is married to his childhood sweetheart, Teana. They share three children and nine grandchildren. He has pastored two congregations: the first for ten years and the second since 1991. He also teaches theology, Bible, and humanities at two universities. His DMin in Pastoral Leadership and Management is from Liberty University, and his PhD in Historical Theology is from the University of Babes-Bolyai in Cluj-Napoca, Romania.

www.10thingsabout.org

To buy quantities of this book at a special rate for bulk use, email
info@greatwriting.org

www.ingramcontent.com/pod-product-compliance
Lightning Source LLC
Chambersburg PA
CBHW070549300426
44113CB00011B/1833